Daybreak!

Radical Hospitality in Action

A Project of Depaul USA

Sharon McElhaney, Editor

Yvonne Gabriel, Artist

Regeneration Writers Press, LLC
Macon, Georgia 31201
2018

Regeneration Writers Press, LLC
1177 Adams Street, Macon, GA 31201

www.regenerationpress.com
editor@regenerationpress.com

ISBN-13: 978-1-945098-01-7

Sharon McElhaney, Editor
Yvonne Maria Gabriel, Artist
Margaret H. Eskew, Publishing Editor
Jerome Gratigny, Technical Editor & Photographer

Editorial Team
Sharon Bailey
Jan Crocker
J. Colin Harris
Duane Evans Davis
Sr. Theresa Sullivan
Diane Lang
Terri DeFoor
Dodie Cantrell Bickley
April Cantrell

All Proceeds from the Sale of This Book Are Donated to Daybreak.

Order Daybreak: Radical Hospitality in Action
from regenerationpress.com
or
amazon.com
or
Regeneration Writers Press, LLC
1177 Adams Street
Macon, GA 31201-1507

Dedication

The Daybreak Community

Sister Elizabeth Greim

Kirby & Joan Godsey

In Memoriam

June Bryant

Al Gerhardt

Denise Saturna

In Gratitude

Depaul USA

"Fill us at daybreak with your love, so that
we can sing for joy as long as we live." Psalm 90:14 (CJB)

Table of Contents

Daybreak is a project of Depaul USA.

DEPAUL
Homelessness has no place

Introduction

by Sharon McElhaney, Editor

A chorus rises from this book, singing the Golden Rule and the inclusion of all in the Beloved Community and touting the power of radical hospitality. Incubated in stories of the Daybreak community, this book shares the joys, creativity, history, work, and challenges of offering radical hospitality in Middle Georgia. It invites all to join the Daybreak community. All contributions of time, talents, gifts, and money swell the chorus of Daybreak, multiplying its reach, its voice, and its beauty.

The portraits of Georgia artist Yvonne Gabriel penetrate our consciousness and connect us on many levels, compelling us to join her on a journey of personal reflection and communion. Kikora S. Chinue, Will Bennett, Pearl Rouise, Jeffrey Carpenter, Graham Knight, and Lisa J. Cannon add earnest Daybreak reflections. Camara Fontenot evokes tragic loss in "The Night Things Fell Apart," and Wilford Campbell dramatically recounts "Going Home." Caroline J. Ivey describes "Outrunning a Tornado," and Diana Snow relates her adventure with "Cats." Daniel Wint reveals a comical "Christmas in Trinidad." "Sue" pieces together the nightmare of her life. Mike Corrigan, Christie Pilcher, and Jeff Battcher affirm the value of volunteering at Daybreak.

Linguist and professor, Margaret Eskew urges us to delve beneath the surface to examine systems at work. Staff member Gaye Martel awakens readers with riveting "Stories of Daybreak." Gaye's "Monday Mornings" gives lie to the traditional dread, revealing that at Daybreak Mondays are more akin to the joy of "coming home." In the "Butterfly Garden, " volunteer Laura Ilan testifies to the lessons of nature and the power that emerges from individuals joining together to work. Among the women who dared to envision Daybreak, Sharon Bailey begins to compile Daybreak's history, weaving various contributors and events together into a beautiful patchwork quilt of vigilant effort, deep commitment to the Beloved Community, and unwavering resolve.

DePaul USA President/Executive Director Charles W. Levesque and Macon Municipal Court Judge and Chair of the DePaul Board of Directors Kathryn W. Gerhardt fit Daybreak into the national perspective, concluding that Daybreak works. In a tribute to Sr. Elizabeth Greim, Joan Godsey convincingly testifies to the difference one person can make. Sr. Katie Norris, the second Daybreak director, identifies what makes Daybreak special, and current Daybreak Director Sr. Theresa Sullivan affirms "The Power of a Village."

Shunning warmed-over platitudes, Mercer Chancellor R. Kirby Godsey gently and eloquently challenges us to rethink our ideas on poverty in "Homelessness: Finding Pathways of Hope." Dr. Godsey lists seven "real and authentic initiatives that we can take toward building bridges of hope between ourselves and the homeless."

The inclusion of different voices allows the notes of each to be heard clearly and distinctly. If we listen intently and with compassion, we can hear this collection of sometimes dissonant voices merge into a truly harmonious chorus unified by the resolve to sing Daybreak everywhere we go.

Daybreak offers radical hospitality.

God is the peace that rises in the early morning with the sunshine—the peace God gives in our hearts and minds. The joy rises in our soul. So, praise the Lord early in the morning. Glorify his holy name.

—Kikora S. Chinue, Community Member

"For I was hungry and you gave me food, I was thirsty and you gave me drink, I was a stranger and you welcomed me ...." Matthew 25:35 (NRSV)

Portrait 1

Daybreak wipes the eyes of the homeless.

Each one of these wonderful people must have been hand-picked to work in concert together, each one having something different to contribute. At Daybreak, they are concerned enough to sit and listen and help figure out what it might be that a person can somehow discover in order to build his faith in God, his confidence in himself, and his trust in those who might attempt to provide assistance.

—Will Bennett, Community Member

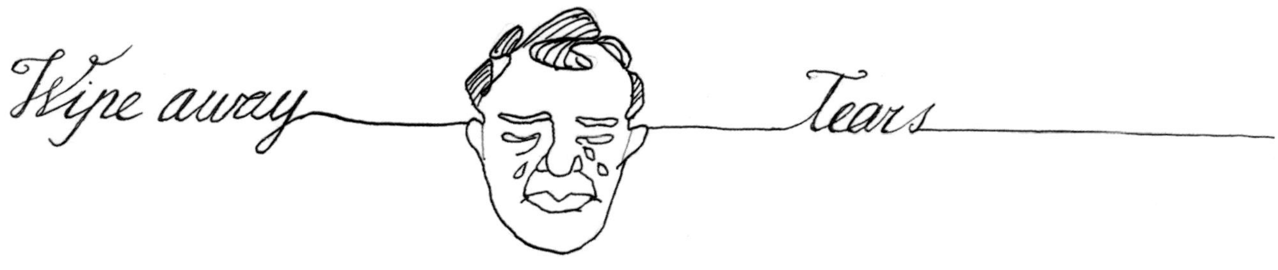

"And God shall wipe away all tears from their eyes ...." Revelation 21:4 (KJV)

Portrait 2

Sr. Elizabeth Greim: Transformer

by Joan Stockstill Godsey

Sr. Elizabeth Greim's impact in Macon, Georgia convinces us that one person can change the world. Through her we learned that communities are not abstract places. Towns and cities have a heartbeat. They are made up of people with faces and names, people who have experienced success and failure, people who know about disappointment and who celebrate gladness.

From time to time, someone enters our lives and captures our hearts with grace and wisdom. For our city, it was Sr. Elizabeth who transformed the tone and character of our life together. She inspired us to see that every person matters, including the broken and the persecuted. She enabled us to understand that lifting somebody up who is beaten down—lifting the powerless—transforms our community into deeper and better places.

Sr. Elizabeth did not teach us about God. She showed us how to become instruments of God. She helped us see the presence of God in people who were forgotten. We have become a community that cares and focuses on lifting people up rather than putting people down. We treasure Sr. Elizabeth's friendship and we deeply love her.

Sr. Elizabeth Greim transformed us.

Choose Daybreak!

by Margaret Eskew

I learned to manipulate the feet, the head, the hands, the knees, and the elbows of my puppets quite adroitly. My puppets could land a punch and smack a kiss, kick a ball, and nod "yes" and "no." My sisters and I would stage puppet fights and puppet love scenes. Our puppets ate and drank, picked blackberries and blueberries, and went to school. We played out the events of our lives through our puppets, sometimes initiating behaviors we knew would not be tolerated at home or school.

At a Mardi Gras parade in New Orleans, grown people vied to catch worthless beads and trinkets. Adults yanked toys from the hands of the intended children. Feet planted themselves on fingers grasping for doubloons. Dollar bills tossed into the crowds transformed ordinarily nice people into greedy monsters. All laws of civility seemed to have been suspended during this time of revelry. Who had masterminded such bedlam?

Elie Wiesel's *Night* depicts life in a Nazi concentration camp. His account of Nazi officials throwing out pieces of bread to watch the starving prisoners fight juxtaposes itself to the Mardi Gras scene. If we just look at those fighting for doubloons or those in the concentration camps grasping for bread, we might be tempted to dismiss the roles of those who orchestrated the events. Are these variations of the puppet show?

We are born into the world with no knowledge of the systems at work. We have to learn how to survive in a world where someone else is pulling the strings even before we know of their existence. There is a tax system at work that few of us have mastered. We know that the highest rate of taxation is on the money we earn by the sweat of our brow, laboring for someone else. The home business tax sits midway between the taxes on interest and dividends and the taxes on our labor. Are we dangling at the end of a string, paying taxes based on rules established to maintain the flow of wealth upward?

Laws are laws, aren't they—impartial rules that all of us must follow? Although we profess to be a country where the law is paramount, we can produce far too many examples where laws have been enacted that benefit the one percent at the expense of the rest of the nation. The administration of justice is green, isn't it? We get just about as much justice as we can afford to pay for. Otherwise, why would our prison system be comprised mainly of the poor and uneducated? Do poor people have a monopoly on crime? Poverty itself has become a crime in some cities. Prisons and poverty work hand in hand to generate more prisons and more poverty. Who benefits from such a system? Following the money identifies those who pull the strings.

The systems under which we operate determine the fate of many. Some of us may become aware of the rules of operation while others have no clue. One disaster victim may qualify for federal aid while another must face rebuilding without outside resources. So what does all of this have to do with homelessness?

There are so many parts of life where we are not in the driver's seat. We can make good decisions, but those decisions do not always insure our wellbeing. Decisions made at the level above us affect our fortunes, sometimes nullifying our well-laid plans. There is a continuing need to revisit our systems to determine whether they are working for the common good. In what ways can we bring about Daybreak for our fellow travelers on the journey?

Some have no clue how to navigate the pitfalls of life successfully. If parents are incarcerated, the odds are that the children will fall into generational poverty. As the writer Richard Rodriguez observed in "The Achievement of Desire," the children of working class families are barely changed by education. Why? Is education failing us? Current economic research supports the existence of the widening gap between the very rich and the middle class and notes that rising out of poverty has become less attainable. Most of us cannot weather great losses. At some level we are all vulnerable even though we have consistently made wise choices.

Daybreak is what it says: the dawning of a new day in a nurturing community. It is a place where those who have been marginalized can reconnect with others as they steady themselves—a place where honest dialogue can happen, and community members can safely enjoy the simple pleasures of life, where we can all witness anew the beauty and resilience of the human spirit.

Even while we work to address the flaws in our systems, we can jealously guard our independence to make the many decisions that remain for us—decisions that can address the inequalities that plague the world and cut the strings that turn us into puppets. Through our decisions, we can provide a safe community such as Daybreak where God's children who have stumbled can regain their balance. Like the Good Samaritan, we can choose to see in each other the image of God.

Choose Daybreak!

Daybreak opens doors that lead to life.

I walked blindly down an ever-deepening spiral, not in touch with reality. My life was not credited with significance. I carried a double load with twice the critique. As I was getting close to that place of no return, someone met me who spoke of a way. I believed in the possibility of that way. Then, being pulled as a fine needle through leather, I made it. Finally, the scales fell off.

—Anonymous

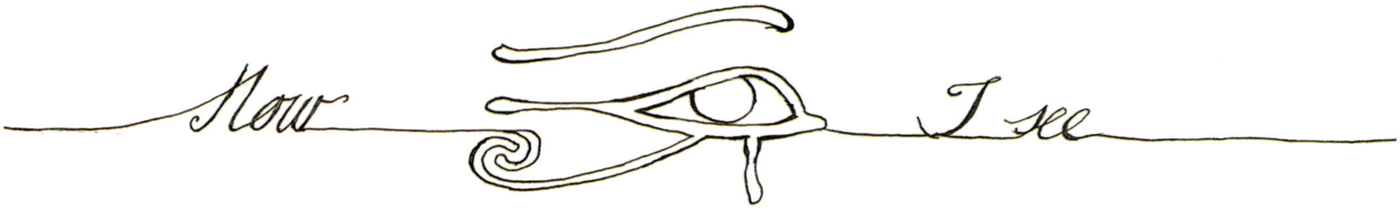

"... one thing I know, that, whereas I was blind, now I see."
John 9:25b (KJV)

Portrait 3

Monday Mornings

by Gaye Martel, Volunteer Coordinator at Daybreak

Monday morning and the alarm wakes you. Maybe you greet it with a groan, a stretch, a little bit of regret that the weekend is over. Perhaps you spent the weekend working in the yard, or baking in your kitchen, or working with your kids on a school project. Maybe you took a family trip. What you know for certain, however, is that today is the day when you return to work, to routine, and with that comes a certain heaviness. Imagine, however, a different scenario, one in which Monday brings relief. Imagine that Monday is the day you get to connect again after a long weekend away from your support system. Imagine that Monday is the day you get to go home.

This is the sense that many of Daybreak's participants have on a Monday morning. People begin to line up at the gate in the dark, waiting for staff to let them onto the grounds of what is, for many of them, the closest thing to home they have known in a long time. The doors open at 7:30 for breakfast, and they file in with their bags and their weariness, thankful for another day at Daybreak. A staff member or volunteer greets each person: "Good morning. I'm glad to see you. Come on in."

In November 2012, Daybreak opened its doors to welcome people living homeless in Macon to a day resource center where they could begin to build lives of stability. The concept was radically simple: (1) offer a welcoming place of rest and invite everyone to come in, the homeless and impoverished, to be served by volunteers; (2) provide basic, critical services such as showers, laundry facilities, and access to telephones and computers; and (3) help build relationships and create community in an atmosphere that fosters respect for all, whether they live in a house or not.

Six years later, Daybreak continues to do just that. Supported by an interfaith group of churches and synagogues, Daybreak excels in accepting people where they are and building trust while they travel towards an independent and positive future. As a project of Depaul USA, Daybreak strategically fills in the gaps in services in Macon, partnering with other organizations to address the needs of the homeless and impoverished.

Daybreak's clinic exemplifies creativity in problem-solving. Through a partnership with Georgia College & State University and First Choice Primary Care, Daybreak meets the medical needs of approximately 130 Daybreak participants per week. Daily medical services at Daybreak and a weekly First Choice clinic enable Daybreak's clients to receive regular and timely care from medical personnel. Their only access previously was the emergency room. They now have access to a health care system enabling them to become medically stable and regularly seen for chronic illnesses.

Daybreak's emphasis on volunteer involvement is another example of creative partnership. Volunteers contribute more than 200 hours a week to the delivery of services such as showers and laundry. Because of its volunteers, Daybreak can offer breakfast four days a week, offer showers to approximately thirty people a day, and help people apply for jobs or write resumes or follow up on benefits applications. Volunteers also come in to socialize, play games, and talk about the weather. It is not always immediately apparent who is a volunteer and who is a participant. Walls come down. Friendships are born. People reconnect to a society that often makes them invisible.

Partnerships make it possible to offer services to help people. Some move into independent lives, and others are simply supported, with dignity, as they struggle. These points of contact create bridges between people, humanize problems, and put a relationship in place where there was once only fear or misunderstanding. Daybreak is a safe space where people put their faith into practice and demonstrate their capacity for love. Monday morning is not a day to dread, but a day to come home.

Daybreak Cares

by Sr. Katie Norris, Director of Daybreak (2016-2017)

Daybreak is a special place where people care about one another. It is a place where people come for breakfast, showers, laundry, and many other services. It is a place of welcome for those who need to get out of the heat or the rain, a place where folks come to relax and look at ways to get their lives back on track. They come to see the nurse. They come because they know someone will care about them. Like the old TV show "Cheers," Daybreak is "a place where everybody knows your name." And if you don't show up for a few days, people wonder and worry and ask questions.

A day shelter is where it began, but a community is what it has become. It is not perfect–what community is? We do our best to work together for the good of the community and we do this through the services provided and through the care and concern expressed each day by those who come through our doors—from the wonderful volunteers and the generous staff to our participants who teach us so much about trusting in the providence of God each day.

The Power of a Village

by Sr. Theresa Sullivan, Director of Daybreak (2017-present)

According to an African proverb, "It takes a village to raise a child." Our need for the village doesn't end with childhood. If we look back, we will see how God has placed people in our lives to encourage and challenge us, and to journey with us. The village supports each of us, and we are called to reach out and support the village. Daybreak's history includes stories that support the importance of the village in developing and sustaining Daybreak. Individuals and groups from many church congregations opened their hearts to allow the Spirit to nudge them to see the plight of people who are homeless. God's people had the courage to learn about poverty and the wisdom to journey with people experiencing homelessness to understand what the needs are. They discovered that being cut off from core village resources contributes to the likelihood of becoming homeless.

The Daybreak Villagers saw the need and shared their gifts. Like the five loaves and two fishes that served 5,000 people with baskets of food left over, the villagers' gifts multiplied under the guidance of Depaul USA to create Daybreak, a respite from the cold, heat, and indifference of Macon streets. Daybreak attests to the power of a village.

Daybreak—a place you call "home."

I dreamt that I went to a place for help. As I entered the building with no clothes on, I had no shame. When it was time for me to be served, the lady didn't notice that I was naked. She thought that I was out of reach with life. No frown was on her face towards me. Nothing.

—Pearl Rouise, Community Member

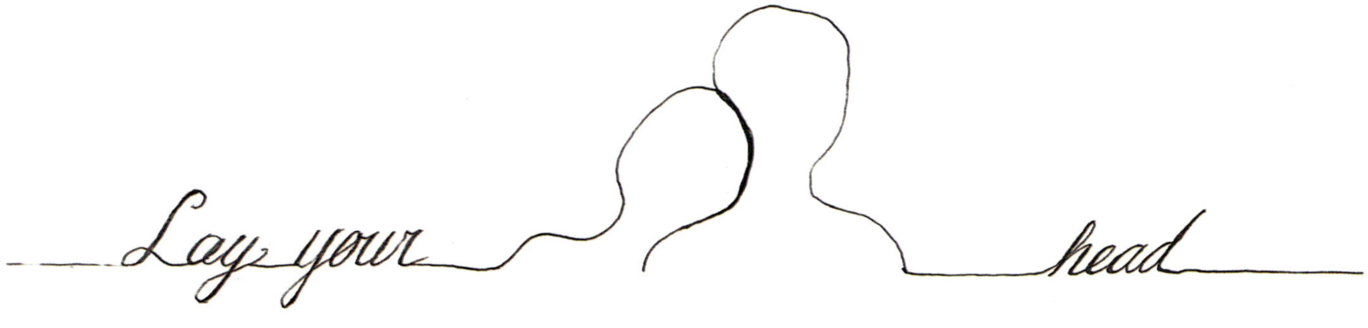

"Foxes have holes, and birds of the air have nests, but the Son of Man has nowhere to lay his head." Matthew 8:20 (NKJV)

Portrait 4

Butterfly Garden at Daybreak

by Laura Ilan, Volunteer

How can something as small and fragile as a butterfly help transform our world? During the summer of 2015 our family toured the beautiful Reiman Gardens located at Iowa State University. What were originally very modest gardens (three-quarters of an acre in 1964) are now a tremendous seventeen-acre community focal point, including a Conservatory Complex and the Christina Reiman Butterfly Wing, which serves as an unofficial welcome mat to the community. I wondered if something like that could happen near Daybreak and Central City Park.

Butterflies are fragile, vulnerable creatures, but also a powerful symbol of renewal and transformation. Daybreak addresses the needs of some of the most fragile and vulnerable members of our community and serves as a place of renewal and transformation for them, as well as for those who support Daybreak's mission. Could butterfly gardens have a transformative influence on Macon?

Over the summer of 2016 six butterfly garden flowerbeds were dug. Family, friends, and Daybreak participants helped plant countless flowers, three potted blueberry bushes, and a small fig tree. It moves my heart and renews my spirit to have Daybreak participants approach me to help in the garden when they are often in need of so much help themselves. Some live in a truck or car, under a bridge, in a tent, or a temporary shelter. In spite of the challenges they face each day, they still take the time to help plant flowers, pull weeds, and water the garden. They always stop to smile, say hello, and express their thanks and appreciation for the flower gardens. This is the Daybreak community.

The Daybreak Butterfly Garden is only a tiny fraction of the original size of Reiman Butterfly Gardens. The Daybreak Butterfly Garden, however, has greatly expanded my connections to those in need as we work together and visit with each other in the garden. The flowers and butterflies serve as a friendly, inviting welcome mat to Daybreak. Working together among the flowers, butterflies, and birds is a therapeutic, meditative exercise, and provides a sense of hope for the future. The flower gardens are a sanctuary for both butterflies and our human spirit and a symbol of both individual and community renewal, transformation, and peace.

Sue's Nightmare

As Told to Sharon McElhaney by an Anonymous Community Member

Sue describes her childhood and teen years growing up in a rural Georgia town in the 1950s and '60s as "third-world living." Her story explains the mental instability that she will probably cope with for the rest of her life. Sue's Navaho Indian mother, Nakita, wisely and skillfully raised and sustained a family of sixteen. They lived in a house made of wood with a tin roof. The walls had holes big enough for the children to look through and tell the time of day, a skill taught to them by Nakita. With no electricity and only a fireplace, Sue remembered always being cold, especially at night.

None of the children attended school regularly. They stayed around the "farm," chopping and carrying wood, and transporting water from the well for cooking, cleaning, washing, and bathing. They swept the grounds, fed the cows, hogs, and chickens, and hunted. Sue and her siblings used their three dogs, Kip, Jerk, and Bobby, to hunt rabbits, squirrels, opossums, turtles, and snakes, which they ate for supper. They were required to pick cotton during the harvest season, put it in a bail, and tie it up. Sue's family never had anything that was store-bought. Everything came from their own land. The family never had visitors and seldom left the farm, except their daddy, William.

William was away from the home most of the time, but when he was there, he verbally, emotionally, and physically abused his family. He refused to upgrade their living conditions. In 1970, Sue and her teenage sisters were sent to live with another family to escape William's abuse. However, in their new home, they suffered the same types of abuse, including rape by the man of the house. Uneducated and untrained, they became mentally deranged as a result of the persistent abuse.

Sue ran away in 1973, pregnant by a young boy in the area. Her life spiraled downhill until she reached rock bottom and was ready to give up. In 1992, three Christians rescued her. Sue found hope in Jesus Christ as her personal Savior. Changed on the inside, Sue experienced the love of God and no longer felt alone.

In 2012, when Daybreak opened, Sue was there, delighting in the love and acceptance of the staff. For Sue, Daybreak is a "relaxation place." Although her medications for mental illness provide some normalcy, she has been unable to find employment. She lives with family and friends and enjoys having time with her grandchildren.

The Night Things Fell Apart

by Camara Fontenot, Community Member

"Bra, Bra. What's wrong with Mama?" I never know what to say when my sisters ask about Mom. I can't explain her condition. Mom used to work. She enjoyed yoga, singing, and dancing. She loved to cook in the wok. Now she sits at the table, reads the Bible, and talks to herself.

Night is when she rages through the house. Her whimpers get louder as her mood changes and like an explosion, screams of rage begin as she races towards the door yelling, "Get out," as if she is chasing someone out of the door. While she stands outside, I see the neighbors turning on their lights. Then the paramedics and police arrive. While they take Mama to the ambulance, the reality of loss is beginning to settle.

The police tell me I have half an hour to say goodbye to my sisters before they take them away. They cry in my arms, "Bra, Bra, we want to stay with you. We love you."

"I love you, too." I feel my heart sinking as I put them in the back of the police car. As the police car drives off, I hear them crying. I have never felt a greater loss. Now I am sitting in this apartment stripped bare of all I know and love.

Daybreak lifts me up.

I sit among strangers, yet we have all things in common—we need shelter, we need family, we need food, we need clothing, we need companionship and care. Daybreak is where we find all of the above. For some, even love and romance can be found.

—Lisa J. Cannon, Community Member

"But thou, O LORD, art a shield for me; my glory, and the lifter up of mine head." Psalm 3:3 (KJV)

Portrait 5

The Story of Daybreak: Piecing Together a Dream

by Sharon Bailey, Volunteer

Like a patchwork quilt, there are many pieces to Daybreak's origin. Central to its creation was Sr. Elizabeth Greim, a Daughter of Charity, who in 2010 was director of Family Advancement Ministries in Macon and a leader in Middle Georgia's organization to end sex trafficking. Following an address by Sr. Elizabeth to Global Women, nine women from neighboring churches came together to explore avenues for service: Sande Day, Dee Bratcher, and Sharon Bailey from First Baptist Church of Christ; Sr. Elizabeth, Candi Michaela, Ramona Mastrangelo, and Maureen Lizak from St. Joseph's; and June Bryant and Tina Clark from High Street Unitarian Universalist Church. Calling themselves Bless These Hands, the group explored the feasibility of working together on community issues. Energized by the success of their joint Fair Trade Festival, the group decided to focus on homelessness in Middle Georgia.

Serendipitously, Sr. Elizabeth traveled to a conference of Vincentian Charities in St. Louis, Missouri, where she chanced to meet friend Chuck Levesque, Executive Director of Depaul USA, a nonsectarian faith-inspired charity founded in 2008 with the mandate from Depaul International to begin five projects to counter homelessness in the USA. Philadelphia had already founded a transitional housing program for men, and New Orleans had developed a transportation assistance program. When asked about Macon, Sr. Elizabeth related the decision of Bless These Hands to address homelessness.

In January 2011 Chuck Levesque met in Macon with about forty representatives of local churches and social service agencies. He outlined the projects of Depaul in Philadelphia and New Orleans and emphasized Depaul's mission to end homelessness. He concluded by offering Macon the opportunity to work with Depaul to become a new resource for the homeless.

Immediately, the assembled group began to list available resources and assess additional needs: emergency housing, food, medical care, shelter from abuse, counseling, IDs, substance abuse, job training and placement, clothing, laundry, showers, etc. The participants developed a dream list for what Macon might offer homeless neighbors, including a building where they could gather during the day. Depaul USA agreed to purchase a building with funds to be repaid as capital funds arrived.

Collaborators came from Baptist, Catholic, Episcopal, Jewish, Methodist, Presbyterian, and Unitarian-Universalist congregations. Civic, business, and community agencies joined the planning efforts. Amazed, Chuck Levesque dubbed the project "The Macon Miracle," testifying that he had never worked with a more dedicated group of volunteers. The spirit of unity across faith traditions energized the group as they worked together toward a common goal.

Denise and Joe Saturna's Sunday evening meal ministry in Central City Park, "Come to the Fountain," provided the venue to involve homeless neighbors in identifying the services they needed: a day center with job placement and training assistance, mental health and other counseling, health care, substance abuse services, day care, GED classes, food, and a place to store personal belongings. The Macon Miracle imagined a day center located near the heart of downtown where individuals could Rest, build Relationships, connect with Resources, and experience Renewal. The center would offer showers, laundry, telephones, computers, and a large day room filled with books, games, and comfortable furniture. There would be classes and counseling served with radical hospitality, a concept developed in the book *Radical Hospitality*, a favorite of Sr. Elizabeth. Goodwill Industries and Central Georgia Technical College committed to job search and training, and the dire need for a clinic was realized.

In November 2011, Daybreak launched a capital campaign to purchase, renovate, and furnish a building on Walnut Street near Central City Park. Volunteers appealed to friends and churches to raise $175,000. Business partners and foundations collected money and donations. Karla Redding-Andrews chaired the campaign. Individual, family, church, foundation, business, and organization gifts far exceeded the goal.

As Daybreak took shape, the vision for additional components expanded, including outside seating and a community garden with a rain-collection system. Architects drew up plans, donors gave furnishings, and construction partners added momentum to the endeavor. Macon Judge Kay Gerhardt and husband Al, a leading Macon contractor, led the renovation. Sr. Elizabeth served as Daybreak's founding director with Denise Saturna as Assistant Director.

On February 20, 2012, Daybreak opened its doors. Community members streamed into the inviting "coffee house" to rest, build relationships, and learn about resources. In summer 2012, Georgia College and State University (GCSU) began exploring with Daybreak the possibility of opening a clinic. In January 2013, the clinic began opening two days a week. Georgia College nurse-practitioner faculty and students provided health care. Dr. Jesse Ray Grant graciously agreed to serve as collaborating physician for the faculty and nursing students. The goal for the clinic was to become the medical home for this population.

All the major equipment in two clinic rooms is on loan from Georgia College School of Nursing. The clinic continues to function today as a clinical training site for Family Nurse Practitioner, Psychiatric Mental Health Nurse Practitioner, and undergraduate nursing students. Drs. Sheryl Winn, Deborah MacMillan, Shannon Merritt, Krystal Canady, Flora Culpa-Bondal, and Dean Baker have worked in the program since its inception.

In 2017, GCSU received a Health Resources Services Administration Training Grant to develop additional partnerships to help train Advanced Practice Registered Nurses to provide care for vulnerable and medically underserved populations. GCSU formed a partnership with First Choice Primary Care and the Georgia Department of Public Health to expand care to include greater access to specialty areas, medical testing, and pharmaceuticals.

In 2016, Sr. Katie Norris succeeded Sr. Elizabeth as director, followed in 2017 by Sr. Theresa Sullivan. With their leadership and the guidance of Depaul, Daybreak has become a vibrant center for building community. The Daybreak family from many faith traditions and community agencies has creatively and beautifully stitched together the pieces of the Daybreak quilt to cover Middle Georgia's at-risk citizens with compassion, generosity, and respect, offering up radical hospitality Georgia-style in downtown Macon.

Daybreak provides a wholesome atmosphere.

Those girls looked so fine at Homecoming, all in a row on the fifty-yard line. It just blows my mind laying here on Recovery Road. No more drugs that's just fine. Hell, yeah, that blows my mind.

—Jeffrey Carpenter, Community Member

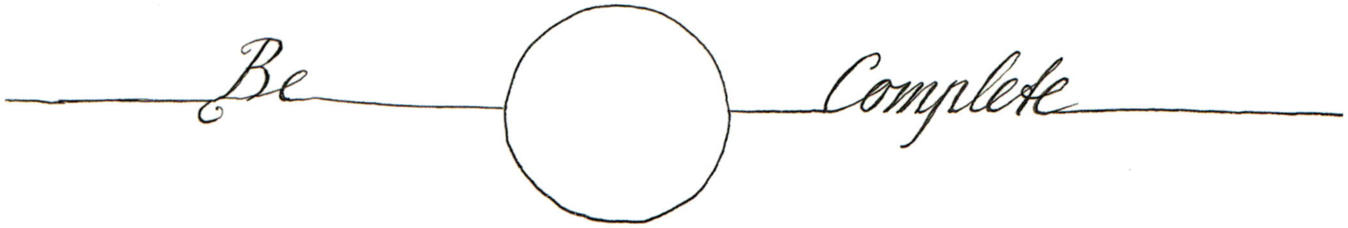

"The LORD is my shepherd; I shall not want."
Psalm 23:1 (KJV)

Portrait 6

You Want Me to Tell You about Daybreak?

by Gaye Martel

The story you want to hear is this:

A man, middle-aged, two weeks out of prison, is sitting in the computer room completing an online job application. I am at the front desk at the other end of the building. An older man built like a boulder and his wiry little friend walk out of a Merle Haggard song and into our building. Dead serious, he says he's here looking for our guy and calls him by name.

I walk him down the hall to the tech room. The two men stand in the middle of the floor, and when our guy looks up from the computer, the older man says, "Come on. Get your things and come get in the truck." Our guy says, "Dad?" like he can't quite believe it, and the little wiry man says, "We came to getcha, Man," with a familiar little laugh that clearly means, "and aintcha a lucky sumbitch because of it." Nobody breaks down and cries or anything, but I've never seen two men so full of emotion they are determined not to show. Our guy doesn't have any things to get. He follows his dad down the hall and out to the truck, and that is that.

It is biblical. It is epic. It is the greatest reunion story I've ever witnessed. And it's the kind of story that makes everyone happy that we do what we do. But here's the part that's harder to tell:

I might have been the first person to talk to our guy when he first came to Daybreak. I was serving coffee at breakfast, and coffee is the first thing most folks do after they come inside in the morning. He was not a likeable guy: pushy, demanding, abrasive. Nothing about him made it easy to want to help him. But Daybreak's mission of radical hospitality demands that I do and insists that I push past what's uncomfortable for me and love harder.

So I do, and other people do, too, and after a couple of days, he mellows into a fairly amiable person. And it becomes clear that, while he is still a pushy, demanding, abrasive guy, the complete insecurity of every aspect of his life had amplified his unsavory traits.

When he came to Daybreak, he had just been released from prison a couple of days earlier. He didn't know where he was going to sleep, if or when he was going to eat, how he was going to get a job, how he could contact his family. He didn't know if his family even wanted him. And at first, they didn't. He didn't know if we were people he could trust to help him, because if a guy's own family quits on him, what's a bunch of strangers gonna do? It is a lonely, terrifying place to be. And Daybreak helps to answer those questions, offers a place where he is welcome, creates a space where he can breathe and begin again.

And it's a great story. Everyone loves that kind of story—the humble lesson learned, the grace, the redemption, the prodigal son and his loving father. But it isn't the usual sort of story. More often than not, it's our guy's family who put his drunk ass on a bus and shipped him south to Macon because they couldn't deal with him anymore. Sometimes, the success story is a long time coming.

> Another ex-felon, and you can tell that this guy had a life-changing experience in prison. He was in for a long time, and he's out on parole, will be on parole for another six years or so. He doesn't let it get him down, though, and he comes into Daybreak with a smile and goes at building his life like gangbusters, starting with the basics: he has to get a birth certificate so he can get a driver's license so he can get a Social Security card so he can apply for a job. All of that takes weeks, months to obtain. But no one can apply for a job anymore without some basic computer skills, and that's not something he learned in prison, so he has to learn that, too.
>
> And I'm not sure if literacy was ever an issue for him, but a high school diploma certainly is, so Daybreak helps him get in a GED program and sets him up with a volunteer tutor. He is so determined and so driven that he requests additional tutoring time and ends up with a second tutor, spending two or three hours a week between the two. All the while, he's keeping up with his multiple appointments: the parole officer, the mental health appointments, the anger management counselors, the required job fairs, the GED class schedule. One missed appointment can mean a punitive unbuilding of all the progress he's made, so he is meticulous about the details of his life.
>
> I watch this man go out into the world every day looking sharp, well-groomed and wearing nice clothes. He is one of the few participants to ever use the iron. He has learned that to be taken seriously he must look serious, so he dresses like a professional to apply for every posted minimum wage job in this city. His prison record prevents him from getting a job offer from a single one of the hundreds of employers he applies to. This goes on for six months—six months of no real reason to believe this is going to get better, six months of pure discouragement. And then, one day, a break comes. Someone takes a chance and says, "Yes." Suddenly, he is employed and owns a car and has a place to live and a girlfriend who becomes his wife. We hardly ever see him anymore, but that's okay.

And that's another one of those success stories people love—the uplifting triumph of determination. It's heady stuff—inspiring. Those aren't my favorite stories, though. In my favorite stories, it's harder to quantify success, harder to put into numbers the data that motivates a donor to give generously. In my favorite stories, the angry man on the street, the homeless guy who bullies all the other people living homeless, learns over time to control his behavior, at least while he's at Daybreak. He learns not to fight when someone looks at him wrong. He learns not to throw people in the river when they make him mad.

In my favorite stories, the smooth-talkin' pimpin' hustler from back in the day wakes up and he's suddenly 61 years old, body failing, mind slipping, illiterate and incapable of working, and it's from that place that he finally experiences true human relationship, learns to lean on people for help, learns to trust that they will care for him, learns about community. He learns that his charm can be simply charming and not just a piece of the hustle.

In my favorite stories, time and time again, people living lonely, isolated lives learn to open up and trust a little. In my favorite stories, homeless people are not the only people the Daybreak experience affects.

A North Macon socialite who volunteers and thinks she's only giving a bit of her time one day knows that she has been giving her heart, too. She knows the names of half of the guys by the fountain. When she goes to eat at the Rookery, she makes eye contact and calls them by name. She smiles and waves and introduces them to her friends—just like they are real people who matter, just like they are all part of the same community—just like that, because they are.

One of our guys is a wolf-born loner. He lives in a tent by the river by choice. He isn't interested in getting help of any kind from Daybreak. He comes to Daybreak for the coffee and the showers and the laundry, and he sits by himself and reads and talks to the three or four people he trusts. A couple of months ago, he started offering to help out. A volunteer couldn't make it to cover one of the stations, and he just offered—like that, out of the blue. It's been ten months since he first started coming in, and the change is very subtle, but perceptible. When someone new is covering that particular station, he'll walk over and check them out, joke around with them, connect with them.

It's maybe a very small thing, but it is just as compelling to me as the story of a father coming to get his son. Both of them are stories about finding a home.

Christmas in Trinidad

Daniel Wint, Community Member

Being from Trinidad in the West Indies means that you grew up on an island where there is no fall or winter season, only the summer and rainy season. Back home, Christmas is a festive season. One of our cultural traditions is called *parang*. The word *parang* derives from the Spanish verb *parrandear*, which means to go out to town to have a good time. And that is just what its music represents. The liveliness of the music is so contagious that it commands a sway. *Parang* is celebrated by festive dress and much good food and drink. The exotic food includes juices, ginger beer, surrol, punchy cream, and rum cake, sometimes called black cake. Families go on extended stays to neighbors' houses to sing songs or speak a message.

This particular Christmas the adults decided to do things a little differently. The young ones would be doing the singing. My uncle and aunt chaperoned us as we headed out to a neighbor's house for *parang* about 5:30 in the evening. Mrs. Rupert, the neighbor, was expecting us and had cleared a space in her dining room, setting up a stage in a corner. The instruments were there: a ukulele, shakers, toc-toc, which is a type of drum, and drums. My uncle struck up the rhythm with the ukulele. The other instrumentalists came in on cue. After he gave us the go-ahead to sing, we all stood there with our mouths wide open. We were so mortified that we could not remember the words to any song, nor did we know what to sing. My uncle started laughing, bowed his head, and walked away. My sister came from behind, grabbed the mic, and blurted out a song she created off the top of her head: "If I did know, if I did know, if I did know Christmas, would I come back?" We looked at each other wondering what the next verse would be. The same words were repeated over and over until the whole gang of children joined in on this simple song. We sang the same verse repeatedly for about an hour.

Thankfully, other parents showed up dressed in red and white Christmas apparel to rescue us. They sang familiar songs that we children knew and could sing with them. They sang about the true meaning of the celebration, the birth of a child that is the Savior of the world. Christmas time has remembrances of home, love, joy, and *parang*.

The Face of Homeless

by Margaret Eskew

What does homeless look like?
Brown eyes? Blue eyes? Green?
Was it just bad choices?
Bad luck? In the genes?

Was it death in the family?
Lost job? A get-rich scheme?
Illness? Drug addiction?
Incarceration? Lost dream?

Betrayal? Separation?
Abandonment? Divorce?
Hurricane? Tornado?
Low wages? No recourse?

Trafficking? Depression?
Parenting concerns?
Just not good with money—
Investment—no returns?

When we look in the mirror
That's where we can see
What homeless looks like—
It looks like you and me.

Daybreak's kindness extends to all.

Homelessness—dreaming dreams of yesterday past. Looking forward to the future in visions of faith. Things hoped for, yet not seen. Watching those who no longer have dreams or visions yet to come. Weeping hearts of lost lives with lost visions of God within, caught in traps running to and fro with no way back and no way forward. Screaming screams of silent, quiet souls.

—Kikora S. Chinue, Community Member

"Because thy lovingkindness is better than life, my lips shall praise thee." Psalm 63:3 (KJV)

Portrait 7

Going Home

by Wilford Campbell, Community Member

One cold New York morning, I asked: "Lord, what am I going to do today?" I loaded clothes to take to the laundry, but instead found myself on the expressway going south with New York City in my rear view mirror. I guess it was about time for me to go home anyway.

On the north side of Atlanta, my SUV started running hot. I pulled into a service station and went inside for a bite. Gathering coffee and snacks, I barely noticed two little girls sitting at a table until one of them shouted, "Hey, he looks like Daddy." I turned to them and asked, "Where are your father and mother?" The biggest girl said, "My daddy out there." I turned to the counter to pay. Suddenly, someone had a choke hold around my neck. I turned around. It was my son.

It had been ten years since I had seen my son. The two girls were my grandchildren. The Lord must have brought me to Georgia for this surprise family reunion in the service station. My son and I rode down the street side by side, as much as possible, laughing and motioning to each other. Just like everybody gathers at a water hole, everybody gathered at my aunt's house. Maybe I had better go away again and come back. This was one of the happiest times in my life.

Modeling Peace

by Christie Pilcher, Volunteer

I first went to Daybreak as a volunteer when only the back part was open. I just sat and knitted, and people would come up and talk to me. Angel even asked me to teach him, and I did. There is a photograph showing how intently he worked at it. Sr. Elizabeth told me once, "You are doing what we want people to do here—and that's to model peace."

Outrunning a Tornado

by Caroline J. Ivey, Community Member

I saw a tornado coming at me. I was holding my baby and ran out the back door down the alley into a ditch about five feet deep. I crawled in a pipe and held my baby out of the water. The tornado sounded like a thousand jets coming overhead. When I crawled out of the pipe, I saw to my right all the apartments on South Zeigler gone. They were gone with the wind. Twenty-two people were killed in Warner Robins, Georgia in 1953. I had a guardian angel. I was covered by the blood of Jesus.

WWJD (What Would Jesus Do?)
HWLF (He Would Love First.)

by Mike Corrigan, Volunteer

I have met so many great people at Daybreak, and they all have a story worth telling. As I share my stories with friends at Daybreak and listen to theirs, one thought permeates my being: There, but for the grace of God, go I. I look forward to every Thursday at Daybreak, meeting new people and marveling at their walk of life and how they quite often do it with a smile, a joke, a hug—even in severe heat and cold.

The hospitality offered at Daybreak truly fills a need, as evidenced by the frequency of its many expressions. The interconnectedness of the services available at Daybreak, Loaves and Fishes, Mulberry Methodist, and the Salvation Army creates a wonderfully effective shelter for Middle Georgia's homeless.

Small Things

by Jeff Battcher, Volunteer

While I was setting up my tent for Daybreak's Sleepout, a gentleman approached me and introduced himself as one of the thankful people who utilizes the services Daybreak provides. His name was Carlton, and his job at Sleepout was to keep the fires going all night. A truck driver in Atlanta, he had gotten into a horrible wreck, lost his home, and eventually found his way to Macon looking for work.

About an hour later I saw him and hollered, "Hey, Carlton! Thanks! The fires look great!" He looked at me and started crying. I asked, "Are you all right? What's the matter?"

"No one's called me by my name in months. When you're homeless, you're a nobody. You get treated like a nobody. It is just so good to hear somebody say my name."

That's what Daybreak is all about. Many times we focus on the big issues, but the vast majority of the time, it's the small things that matter—something as simple as showing someone else the dignity of saying his name.

Cats

by Diana Snow, Community Member

I found a white stray cat in an alley behind the Krystal on Riverside. I found her and brought her home. She was solid white. Shortly, she multiplied into nineteen cats. I ended up taking two litters off and leaving them because I could not take care of them.

Daybreak listens and understands.

Charlie Jr. dropped over in a certain part of the ditch, a sink-hole. It sucked him under. I can still see him spinning around and around going down. One of the other guys hollered, "He's drowning; he's drowning." Another friend extended a stick, but Charlie Jr. could not reach it. He was swirling in the water. I could not save him. He died.

—Will Bennett, Community Member

"He administers justice for the fatherless and the widow, and loves the stranger, giving him food and clothing." Deuteronomy 10:18 (NKJV)

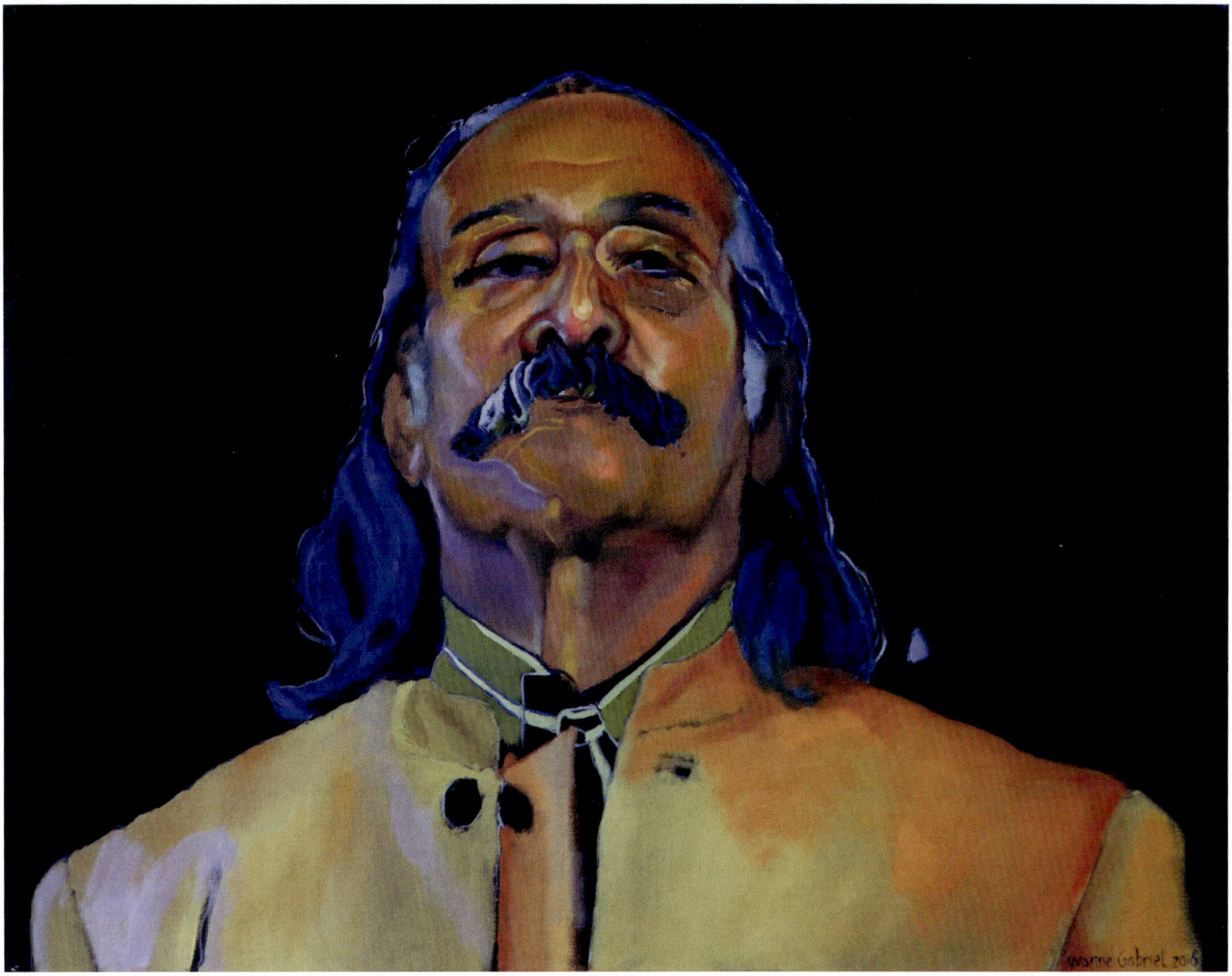

Portrait 8

"Behold the fowls of the air: for they sow not, neither do they reap, nor gather into barns; yet your heavenly Father feedeth them. Are ye not much better than they?"
Matthew 6:26 (KJV)

Daybreak is a refuge to those in need.

Daybreak is my shelter from a troubled highway of life. Having been made homeless through no fault of my own, I found that Daybreak helped me come to terms with my lot. It supplies me with shelter from the elements throughout the days, gives me laundry facilities, a shower, Internet and telephone access, snacks and breakfast, and most of all, help with finding medical assistance.

—Graham Knight, Community Member

"God is our refuge and strength, a very present help in trouble." Psalm 46:1 (KJV)

Portrait 9

Homelessness: Finding Pathways of Hope

by Dr. R. Kirby Godsey, Chancellor, Mercer University

Far too often we confuse being homeless with being "houseless." Homelessness is more than being without a house. It might better be described as life in a barren desert. All across our land, there exists a burgeoning plague of homelessness that is symptomatic of a much deeper social ill. It tears at the soul of our culture and diminishes our communities. When we examine homelessness, we find that people often feel hopeless before they become homeless. Reaching that dark and empty place sustains and deepens the loss of hope. Without hope, we can only exist; we do not live. If we are to address seriously the problem of homelessness, we, as communities and societies, will have to see it as our problem, not "their" problem. As we face this growing problem, our challenge is whether we can define and implement pathways of hope.

While we should never discount the importance of shelter, homelessness is both an inward and outward experience. At the outset, we should establish more systematic and comprehensive ways to provide outward shelter. Shelter is too episodic and inconsistent. And, shelter alone will not alleviate the tragedy of being homeless. Homelessness includes and often springs from a sense of isolation, a sense of being cut off from the moorings that give purpose and character to our lives. Providing a meal and a bed satiates but does not restore that sense of purpose or wellbeing. While homelessness refers to the trap of being without shelter, it also speaks to the conditions of a larger society that copes with the reality of the homeless by profiling them into a category of people alien to us. We want the homeless to remain people who live outside our boundaries. We want to keep them in their place, curtained off from mainstream society. It is a modern-day caste society in which we regard the homeless to be an outside, even outcast, class from which we wish to remain distant, separate, and superior.

We are reluctant to entertain the notion that their being homeless is intimately connected to us and to our own human condition. In order to absolve our "dis-ease," we put a dollar in the hat. We offer five dollars for a meal while expecting that it may be used for booze. Giving the dollar or five dollars or twenty dollars is not a way of engaging; it is a symptom of disengagement. Our giving is not so much for them as it is for us. It may alleviate a hidden sense of guilt for our social dysfunction. It is also our way of touching the untouchables in a manner that keeps them at an appropriate distance.

So, the question arises, "Are they—the outcasts, the street people—really more homeless than we?" We have physical houses, but we also live in community silos that protect us from one another. We can live in our neighborhoods and be as isolated as the homeless. Like them, we too often live with the aim of making it one more day, being kept alive by the noise and the machinations of work and play. But when the light grows dim and silence prevails, are we really any different? Do we live with a stronger sense of purpose? Do we live less isolated lives?

To address the challenge of homelessness, we have to begin with our common humanity. Our wellbeing is interwoven with their wellbeing. Our lives overlap. While it may be more comfortable to live in our isolated cells called neighborhoods, where we may not even know our neighbors, we belong to one another because we are members of one common family. There is no hope for the homeless or ourselves until we accept the reality of our interior connectedness.

To address homelessness, we have to work harder to understand the contrasting territories in which we live. We have to find new ways to bridge the divide that haunts our social condition and the social illness that leads to homelessness. Those who live on the street and those who live in gated territories have far more in common than they have in distinction. We are bred of the same biology and the same chemistry. The tragedy of the homeless ripples through our own social being. Their dislocation is a symptom of our own.

Social distance and physical distance from one another are both a choice and an assignment. Some people choose to live on the street because they provide a place of social acceptance. Some people choose to live in gated enclaves because they also convey a sense of social acceptance. Society assigns the poor to the street either literally or figuratively. The rich are assigned to their gated community. Each, to some measure, is driven by fear of one another. Our social and physical distances are more often than not defined by fear. The rich are afraid of the poor. The poor are afraid of the rich. Those in homes are afraid of the homeless, and the homeless are afraid of persons who live in remote houses. Fear breeds isolation. Isolation breeds contempt, and contempt breeds hostility.

In our view of the homeless, negativity usually prevails. How do we regard the homeless? Let us count the ways. They are lazy. They are dirty. They are prone to crime. They are mentally ill. They abuse drugs and alcohol. They are unfit. They are rips in the social fabric. Negativity breeds negativity. The homeless view those who ride by in their closed cars and reside in remote neighborhoods as arrogant, uncaring, condescending, suspicious, stingy, and thoughtless. Negativity, an outcome of social circumstance defined by fear, breeds greater and greater social exclusivity. We become citizens of a land foreign to one another.

Building bridges between the rich and poor is very difficult, in part, because our self-protective instincts cause us to rush to judgment toward one another. Prejudices run deep. But while building new bridges does not necessarily require that we change our judgment, it does require that we be willing to suspend our judgment in order to consider alternatives.

In this state of suspended judgment, our chief goal is not to learn a new set of facts. The fact of homelessness is self-evident. But neither our life nor theirs is made up mostly of facts. The real challenge of bringing hope to the homeless is to become willing to listen to their stories. It is true of rich and poor, true of those who live in houses and those who live "under the bridge." Each one of us has a story. There are no homeless persons who do not have a story. They did not suddenly appear on the street. Their story is a human story. Each one of us has a face and a name and a history. The homeless and the well-to-do were born somewhere and were born to someone. They were suckled by a mother. They have a father who is either present, or barely present, or absent altogether. They began to see a world that is full of light and shadows, hurt and pleasures, caring and conflict. We and they share a common humanity, and that common humanity is awakened by stories. You and I belong to that common humanity. We did not abruptly wake up in a gated community. Our being where we are comes with a story. The story of the homeless is no less human than the story of the social elite.

The substructure of every bridge between rich and poor, between the homeless and the well-to-do, is always built around a story. None of us appeared out of nowhere. We all have a history. And there will be no recourse for the homeless dilemma unless we are willing to look deep within our own histories and our own stories. Every person's story is a sacred trust and every person's story is deeply personal. You cannot know me without knowing my story. You cannot help me without hearing my story.

Categorizing people as lazy or ne'er-do-wells, as reprobates and abusers, is an easy way to reject the homeless story. There is no salve that can heal our divided selves. Every homeless person, because of our common humanity, is connected to every person living in a safe and secure house. Our human biographies are profoundly interwoven, and the ultimate difference between us becomes almost trivial. Shelter or the lack thereof is a fleeting characteristic of the human condition, rather than a defining component of the human situation.

Homelessness indicates that as a society, as a human community, we are still in the process of becoming civilized. After all, civilization is yet in its infancy, and homelessness is a holdover of our barbarian beginnings. If we are to advance civilization, we should not rest with the incivility of human disrespect that we call homelessness. It is evidence of the chaos that continues to persist within our human order.

We need a new starting place, and the new starting place to which we should surrender is that no person can be fully at home as long as one person is homeless. No person can be fully rich as long as one child goes to bed hungry. We will either shape our human destiny together, or our fractured and divided civilization will sink more deeply into the decay that leads to bitter disorder.

Our most pressing challenge is to construct a pathway of hope for both the homeless and those of us who live in insulated segments of society that are defined by material possessions. In the end, neither they nor we possess anything. Possession is a siren call that will ultimately abandon us. The good for which we all must reach is not possessions, but hope. Possessions alone will leave us hopeless. Hope, more than possessions, is our life source. The underlying challenge for all of us, rich or poor, homeless or well-housed, is whether our human condition precipitates a descent into hopelessness. Hopelessness is our common human threat. Hopelessness is the urgent challenge of the homeless and also the challenge of the cloistered rich. Hopelessness is not bound by place, or social or financial status. If we have the courage to provide a pathway of hope for the homeless, we may find new light of hope for ourselves.

In order to define that path of hope, we must identify some realistic steps that we can take that will ignite the embers of hope to be rekindled among those who are the victims of homelessness. Doing so can also become a reservoir of hope for those who live with hopelessness behind closed doors. There are real and authentic initiatives that we can take toward building bridges of hope between ourselves and the homeless.

Seven Steps to Building Bridges of Hope

1. Caring for the homeless and helping them discover horizons of hope always begin with listening. If we are not prepared to listen, we will rarely become a vehicle of hope. We must begin with this understanding: Every person counts. Every person matters. There are no unimportant people in the world, including the powerless. Every person has a story that deserves to be heard.

Help does not begin by giving instructions; it begins by being silent. Listening, above all else, is the most elementary form of respect. It is empty to say to someone that you respect them but are unwilling to listen to them. We should also understand that listening is far different from allowing another person to talk as our minds wander away. Listening means active, personal engagement. It may be painful. It is certainly hard work. It requires patience and caring and it can be emotionally exhausting. Listening does not mean agreeing with all you are hearing, but every human being deserves the respect of a listening ear. If we want to help the homeless find a path of hope, we must be prepared to translate caring into thoughtful and respectful conversation. Listening and dialogue, rather than preachments, will point the way.

Homelessness is not a destination; it is a detour signaling that someone has lost his way. We can only rekindle the fire of hope by taking each person seriously and hearing about their journey to this place. Hope begins by being present.

2. Bringing hope to the homeless means helping them find a foothold for beginning to believe in themselves again. The loss of self-esteem pervades the consciousness of the homeless, the powerless, and sometimes the powerful as well. Believing in ourselves can be shattered in legions of ways. It may be the rejection of parents, a sense of abandonment by peers, the experience of abuse, or a crippling loss of work.

   Relating to others effectively always begins with believing in ourselves. If we do not believe in ourselves, we will never believe in another. We live in a culture that finds subtle ways of putting one another down. If we are put down long enough, we begin to believe that we are worthless. Regaining self-respect, believing again in our value as human beings, often requires the encouragement that only another person has the capacity to give. Helping people regain the gift of self-respect and self-confidence provides a pathway for finding hope amidst a journey that has tumbled into despair. Helping persons find a foothold means providing the kind of space and human connectivity to begin to see themselves in a new light. A meal to eat, a bed for sleep, a counselor to listen and to help reimagine their identity can become a path toward hope.

3. Building bridges of hope requires that we earnestly confess and face up to the social ills that contribute to homelessness and undergird it in its utter sense of isolation. In America, we live in an increasingly troubled society, divided by ideology and race and the widening gap between the "haves" and "have-nots." The polarizations in our society have likely never been greater. Beyond being divided, we face the danger of becoming closed islands of diverse thinking. Leaders talk past one another. Democratic societies are built on trust in the power of freedom and reason. The founders of this republic believed that free people could make rational choices—choices that were often the outcome of vigorous debate. Closed sub-societies within our republic are a rejection of the power of thought and collaboration and the vision-creating power of debate and reason. Closed societies believe they have the absolute answers that they believe absolutely.

   If we are to overcome the ill of homelessness, we must be prepared to open ourselves to contrary viewpoints and to work within that diversity to find common ground. Otherwise, our divide only becomes deeper, and we remain captives who live on islands of absolute opinion. This social ill of absolutism and exclusivity breeds darkness, not light. The path of hope requires opening our minds and hearts to people whose life experience is drastically different from our own. Hope lies in creating connectivity within a thoughtful and respectful society that values diversity and believes that every person has the potential to add value.

4. Overcoming the plague of homelessness requires that we take on the challenge of pursuing active and realistic solutions to poverty. Poverty is not the only source of homelessness. Even so, our social tolerance of poverty contributes to our willingness to ignore the challenge of homelessness. "The poor and the homeless we always have with us" may be true, but it should not lead to "washing our hands" of any responsibility for these social ills.

   The most important tool for addressing the problems of poverty is education. Yet, in fact, children born into poverty may be lost to an educated future long before they enter schooling years. The number of children born into poverty is finite, and we, for our own wellbeing and the hope for a civil society, must intervene and insure that even the poorest of the poor are prepared to learn. Learning is the principal means of breaking the bonds of poverty. The pathways of hope will require that we become increasingly engaged in overcoming the ravages of poverty. None of us is rich as long as one of us is hungry and neglected and unsheltered. Our futures are intertwined. Homelessness is a symptom of the scourge of poverty. Unless we become more focused on addressing poverty, we will lose the battle against homelessness.

5. Constructive pathways of hope also begin with the recognition that the homeless are full members of the human family. The homeless are not outside society. When we lose one person to poverty or homelessness, we are diminishing our capacity for human progress. Every individual, including the homeless and the derelict, can bring clear and certain gifts that are locked away in the travail of homelessness. Every person is a universe of one. Each one can see what has never been seen, dream what has never been dreamed, say what has never been said, do what has never been done.

   When a homeless person loses hope, the whole of society suffers. The world will never have the advantage of what that one person could have contributed. It leaves an empty place on the human roster that will never be filled. The human family needs the value that every member can contribute. The well-homed and the homeless all belong to one human race. Our highest victories lie in reclaiming every ray of light that each person can bring. We are too inclined to set the homeless aside as a useless and irrelevant component of the human family. The loss of one person to poverty or ignorance or drug abuse reverberates through all our lives. The suffering of one diminishes the hope of all.

6. Building pathways of hope also includes the reality that we must cultivate a community commitment to shelter the homeless and to create a safe place where they may recover a better glimpse of the person they can become. We should not doubt that it is useful to shelter and feed the homeless, while understanding that sheltering and feeding are a platform, not a solution. They are a beginning,

not an end. Shelter and food alone will not guarantee sustainable hope. Hope is born when we create places and experiences where the homeless can gain a new understanding of themselves and have the assistance to help them craft a new future. They must find the space to see themselves beyond the travail of being homeless, a place to reimagine their lives, to regain a sense of self-worth and to design a pathway toward wholeness.

7. The pathway toward hope always points forward. A part of being trapped by the plague of homelessness that leads to sustained hopelessness lies in allowing ourselves to become stranded in yesterday. We become consumed by yesterday's disappointments. We become a victim of yesterday's bad choices and yesterday's hurt. Life in the rear-view mirror is an illusion. The way home beyond the haunting presence of yesterday is to live forward. The way to a new day is to let go of yesterday. The present day is the only day that has a heartbeat. We cannot allow our lives to be defined by yesterday's defeats or yesterday's broken promises.

   The homeless and those who live in gated silos of security must learn that we have to let go of what might have been and grab hold of what is yet possible. Too often the homeless and even the cloistered well-to-do are drowning in yesterday's mistakes. Finding hope means letting go of the past and reimagining our future. The task of all who care about the homeless is to help them come to terms with the present—to catch a compelling sense of what is yet possible and to gather the tools, skills, and self-confidence to translate the possible into the actual.

If any community is to achieve its own highest potential, we cannot simply ignore the homeless as outcasts. We have to be realistic people of hope who believe in the homeless as valued members of our community. We must help them gain the physical and mental care that enables them to climb beyond the drought of existence by which they are defining their lives. It is our own sense of hope that enables us to embrace the homeless, becoming flesh-and-blood hope for them. Everyone of us is somebody's best hope. Every homeless person is a person who has somehow lost his or her way. Becoming somebody's hope, helping find a new way, will help us find our own way. As human beings, we find hope by becoming hope.

The blight of homelessness will require the investment of financial resources. Our overcoming this social ill will be costly; not doing so will be more costly. Of course, we should recognize that financial resources alone will not be sufficient to cure this haunting dilemma. We cannot buy our way out of this situation. Hope for the homeless requires human intervention because hopelessness is more deadly than homelessness.

Our highest calling is to become the embodiment of hope by being present and by building and refining and sustaining social systems of hope that affirm the worth of every person. Our mission must be to overcome homelessness by creating compelling pathways of hope. Our mission is to see that the homeless do not view their plight as a destination, but an interlude for rebuilding a future with new promise. There is no external cure for homelessness. Homelessness is not a problem we can fix from the outside. It is an interior problem that requires human engagement. We have to provide settings and environments and human interactions where the homeless can reimagine themselves as persons who can themselves become instruments of hope and light in the world.

The human race is fragile. Homelessness is a witness to the failure of human community. We cannot overcome that failure without building pathways inclusive of all people, all genders, all races, all ethnicities because our hope is completely interdependent. We ignore the challenge of homelessness at great peril. But peril need not be our final word. Homelessness is a human problem susceptible to the human will and human initiative. Our commitment to civility can bring us to the threshold of a commitment of will and initiative. The advance of our communities and our civilization cannot abandon some of the human family. We face a shared future, for we are threads in one common human fabric.

Joy Lynn Smith Stanley, Artist
Macon, Georgia

The artist portrays the Daybreak building as an upbeat and action-filled place where hope and healing begin.

Daybreak is acceptance.

Daybreak is the joy of the early morning after sleeping under bridges and places no one would go. Daybreak is the warmth of my shower—the cleansing of my soul, reminding me that I am still the son of God. My heart is touched not to give up, that homelessness is a trial and tribulation.

—Kikora S. Chinue, Community Member

"Fill us at daybreak with your love, so that we can sing for joy as long as we live." Psalm 90:14 (CJB)

Portrait 10

DEPAUL

Homelessness has no place

Depaul USA: Mission, Vision, & Values

Depaul USA aims to end homelessness and change the lives of those affected by it. Programs serve those who are materially poor, treating participants with dignity and respect, and providing counseling. All of our programs have the same overarching goals: to help homeless men and women overcome the immediate crisis of homelessness, to help participants become economically more self-sufficient, to enable participants to improve their health and well-being, and to help participants attain and maintain housing.

Depaul USA envisions a society in which everyone has a place to call home and a stake in his/her community.

Depaul USA owes its inspiration and its Values to Vincent de Paul, a major social reformer in 17th Century France. Vincent de Paul reached out to the poor and the disenfranchised, valuing each and every person. He attracted a large group of supporters and volunteers, whom he inspired with his love for the poor, building bridges between rich people and those living in poverty. Macon is one of six cities where Depaul offers programs.

Homelessness has no place in Macon, Georgia.